First Adam vs. Last Adam

America's Tale of Two Kingdoms

Angie

Vote For The Kingdom

Enjoy
Rod Hemphill

First Adam vs. Last Adam

America's Tale of Two Kingdoms

Rodney Alan Hempel

ELM HILL

A Division of
HarperCollins Christian Publishing

www.elmhillbooks.com

First Adam vs. Last Adam
America's Tale of Two Kingdoms

Published in Nashville, Tennessee, by Elm Hill, an imprint of Thomas Nelson. Elm Hill and Thomas Nelson are registered trademarks of HarperCollins Christian Publishing, Inc.

Elm Hill titles may be purchased in bulk for educational, business, fund-raising, or sales promotional use. For information, please e-mail SpecialMarkets@ThomasNelson.com.

Library of Congress Cataloging-in-Publication Data

Library of Congress Control Number: 2019913425

ISBN 978-1-400328895 (Paperback)
ISBN 978-1-400328901 (Hardbound)
ISBN 978-1-400328918 (eBook)

DEDICATION

*This book is dedicated as a memorial to my grandfather,
Herman Morris Kohl, born in Vienna, Austria on April
1, 1895. Born of Jewish parents, Leib and Marjem Kohl,
and circumcised on April 28, 1985 of record dated June
30, 1985. He emigrated to America arriving on October 2,
1912 from Bremen, Germany on the vessel Hanover. He
married Martha Sperber on June 17, 1916 in Philadelphia
and settled in Elizabeth, New Jersey. Herman
passed on February 19, 1962.
He became a Christian citizen of the Kingdom Of God.*

ACKNOWLEDGMENTS

For over twenty-five years, the Ellicott City Assembly of God has encouraged me to teach Adult Bible Study; I thank the members of this study for their words of support. I thank my dedicated Christian wife, Rachelle, for her steadfast belief in Jesus. And I thank God for the insight and opportunity to speak this message.

TABLE OF CONTENTS

CHAPTER 1

What Two Kingdoms?

A Heavenly Kingdom Messenger Arrives

There are a vast number of Americans, as well as, citizens of every country that voluntarily recognize two distinct governments, or kingdoms, that share authority over their daily lives. These citizens desire dual authority to give them balance. Vice versa, both governments declare to their citizens that they have a valid right to share authority over their fellow citizens. Let's identify these as the national governments established by mankind, which are upon earth, whereas, the other government derives power from a heavenly and spiritual realm.

It's obvious to everyone that all nations already have an autonomous and sovereign governmental authority over their citizens. Some governed citizens of nations, respectfully, decide to submit to another government that claims a higher heavenly authority that is not of this world. These people become dual citizens, so to speak. Indeed, they are seeking something that their fellow national citizens do not.

If a significant portion of a nation's citizens believe that there exists another kingdom government that originates in the heaven, the national government should seek to accommodate their view of a higher authority. By acknowledging their people's belief, a nation can make accommodations in order for all citizens to live together peaceably. Good and wise government comes from respect for considering an opponent's viewpoint. There is validity in listening to alternative ideas and the best law and ideas result.

If the national government is wise, its policy would be to encourage its citizens to respect one another's established religious rights. Folks need to become tolerant of the higher authority expressed in religious viewpoints. And, the national government should endorse a policy of religious free choice. As Americans, our national government does indeed assure every citizen religious rights.

It becomes troubling when a nation's citizens become heatedly divided about yielding to the authority of another higher kingdom. Especially since recognizing a heavenly authority is a voluntary choice of many citizens. What an opportunity for confusion and conflict among citizens! This is a picture of America today in conflict. From where does this have its beginning?

The American Christian acknowledges that the spiritual authority in their lives originates over 2000 years ago. It is best described by the famous conversation between Jesus and a Jewish Pharisee named Nicodemus. It's an encounter where Jesus says that he has been sent by his Father to announce that he has been granted authority from the Father to form a new spiritual kingdom upon earth, which has the absolute highest authority to govern our lives!

This higher authority is superior to all existing religious practices, as well as superior to all national governments. What an audacious statement! Let's begin with a slow read of this announcement of this kingdom authority revealed by the Lord Almighty's messenger, this Jesus, who claims to be both the Son of God and also the Son of Man (mankind).

FROM JOHN 3:1–3:

Now there was a Pharisee, a man named Nicodemus who was a member of the Jewish ruling council. He came to Jesus at night and said, "Rabbi, we know that you are a teacher who has come from God. For no one could perform the signs you are doing if God were not with him."

Jesus replied, "Very truly I tell you, no one can see the kingdom of God unless they are born again."

So, the takeaway from the viewpoint of Jesus is that there is another kingdom. It's God's kingdom. And, a person cannot see it unless a certain second birth occurs. And God has sent his messenger who wants us to experience it and to learn about it. What type of birth is required to be a citizen of God's kingdom? Jesus explains clearly.

From John 3:5–8:

Jesus answered, "Very truly I tell you, no one can enter the kingdom of God unless they are born of water and the Spirit. Flesh gives birth to flesh, but the Spirit gives birth to spirit. You should not be surprised at my saying, 'You must be born again.' The wind blows wherever it pleases. You hear its sound, but you cannot tell where it comes from or where it's going. So it is with everyone born of the Spirit."

We can enter this kingdom by doing two simple things. First by repenting from whatever way that we are following and earnestly begin focusing on becoming more aware of this new type of kingdom. We need an open mind. Like water flowing toward a new direction, a baptism into a new direction is needed. Minds need to be fluid and must consider that God is moving in a new direction. Exploring this new covenant direction is required in order to discover this kingdom. And then second, somehow citizens must be imparted Spirit from the kingdom itself.

There is an important distinction to be made, that citizens of the kingdom of God must be born of water and, of Spirit; not of water and religion.

Becoming a kingdom of God citizen then involves a two-step process. It is a voluntary two-part covenant between a citizen who actively and wholeheartedly seeks God's kingdom, and then a response by his acceptance into God's kingdom confirmed by being given Spirit from God through his Son, Jesus. So, Jesus is the gatekeeper of God's kingdom and this must be believed by those entering in. There is an initial seeking action and then a response confirming heavenly citizenship.

FROM JOHN 3:11–15:

"Very truly I tell you, we speak of what we know, and we testify to what we have seen, but still you people do not accept our testimony. I have spoken to you of earthly things and you do not believe; how then will you believe if I speak of heavenly things? No one has ever gone into heaven except the one who came from heaven—the Son of Man. Just as Moses lifted up the snake in the wilderness, so the Son of Man must be lifted up, that everyone who believes may have eternal life in him."

At last, it becomes clear that there is a heavenly kingdom and it is clearly revealed to us! One earthly—a national government—and one heavenly! And dual citizenship is offered to those who chose to believe in Jesus. A good question to ask would be whether these two kingdoms operate in concert with one another, or do they oppose one another? Does the heavenly kingdom express authority over the national one? Yes, but the national authority is never usurped, it is much needed.

From John 3:16–21:

For God so loved the world that he gave his one and only Son, that whoever believes in him shall not perish but have eternal life. For God did not send his Son into the world to condemn the world, but to save the world through him. Whoever believes in him is not condemned, but whoever does not believe stands condemned already because they have not believed in the name of God's one and only Son. This is the verdict: Light has come into the world, but people loved darkness instead of light because their deeds were evil. Everyone who does evil hates the light, and will not come into the light for fear their deeds will be exposed. But, whoever lives by the truth comes into the light, so that it may be seen plainly that what they have done has been done in the sight of God.

This heavenly kingdom is being offered as an opportunity to have both an eternal life and an abundant one here and now! It simply depends upon believing that God is reconciling people to him through Jesus. So, God having sovereign authority over all creation is now making an extraordinary offer of peace. He is offering to all mankind a superior government that outlasts a person's life in the natural worldly kingdom. An offer of reconciliation has been extended to become a citizen of heaven through believing in the Son of God, Jesus. We are no longer barred from entry in God's kingdom. We choose to voluntarily enter his eternal kingdom. A far better government filled with boundless opportunity to bless its citizens! Jesus is charged with revealing it to us with the help of his Father. Clearly, two kingdoms and two governmental authorities have been revealed.

CHAPTER 2

COMING TO AMERICA

The Declaration of Independence

S ince this declaration of a heavenly kingdom, some 2000 years have passed. Many people all over the world have become not only citizens of their independent nations, but also citizens of God's heavenly kingdom, living as dual citizens.

Some of the most extraordinary were a few fellows who were given the privilege to form a new national government. In what was a provident moment, they obligated the new government to serve and protect not only the rights granted to their nation's citizens, but also their new nation would yield to the rights of citizens of God's supreme kingdom. They thought that national government authority should always consider the purposes of God and, therefore, should accommodate not only their governing stewardship of national citizens but also their dual citizens. Both folks could live out their lives in the pursuit of life, liberty, and the pursuit happiness. Makes one think of the words used in the United States Declaration of Independence:

> *"We hold these truths to be self-evident, that all men are created equal, that they are endowed by their Creator with certain inalienable rights, that among them are Life, Liberty and the pursuit of Happiness."*

This is a clear statement that acknowledges two kingdoms, a national one and a heavenly one. The declaration of the new American nation that is about to be formed must assure their citizens, that governmental leaders will use their authority to protect the rights of citizens of God's kingdom. Quite a unique viewpoint as opposed to the will of a national sovereign king who has been invested with Divine power to decide the rights of citizens. New American citizens will be set free to pursue their God-given opportunities and blessings. And America, by doing that, became the undisputed leading country in the world!

So, the traditional viewpoint that has been established is that the men who instituted our American government thought that they derived their authority from God. They were establishing a government to protect rights given by a Creator to all men.

Before our Constitution was written, Americans

fought the Revolutionary War to secure their God given rights.

These founding stewards were fifty-six in number, and all understood that there really are two kingdoms that coexist and people can acknowledge both kingdom authorities! Both kingdoms promoting similar causes that are viewed as right and just. Each working in concert trying to serve their citizens' needs.

Certainly, there have been periods when differences between these two kingdoms arise and challenge how national authority is to be executed. There has always been an epic struggle for national supremacy over the heavenly kingdom. Kind of sounds like the modern American storyline.

Will citizens of today's modern-day national kingdom continue to tolerate others who also follow their traditional faith in the heavenly kingdom? There is the possibility that this viewpoint simply doesn't satisfy the majority of American citizens anymore. Folks in the heavenly kingdom should yield their faith only to the national government. "Bless their hearts. Poor souls. They just aren't up to modern times. Wish they could see the light!"

Unfortunately, it seems that the goal of the American modern-day government is to always be putting pressure on its citizens to fundamentally change from the original founders' viewpoint. American government today is assuming the role that it alone is sufficient in determining all rights of citizens, and even to define and pronounce new rights to its citizens and even illegal residents. To abandon the fundamental guiding principles, and therefore explaining that it is unfair that some citizens thrive and some do not. Perhaps some are blessed by God for their faith. No matter, the tendency is to ignore and to override the kingdom of God's dual role in governing.

Today, our American government assumes the duty to define mandatory laws on what will become the standard for righteous behavior among its citizens. Our national government is determined to correct every perceived injustice. Today, rights can now only be granted by the American government. When there are conflicting issues, the first Adam, the rule of mankind, now requires that God's kingdom take a backseat. There is now a great gulf between the signers of the Declaration of Independence and today's First Adam government that arrogantly steps in and always knows right from wrong. First Adam government claims be uniquely competent to decide how to provide life, liberty, and the pursuit of happiness without any need to seek assistance from the superior wisdom of the heavenly kingdom of God.

Today's American citizen can now do it alone and do what is right in their own minds on every issue of gender, abortion, income equality, immigration, foreign policy, tax policy, environmental policy, education, poverty, climate change, racial equality, and so forth. American leaders are showing bitter uncompromising partisan intolerance. And they lecture its citizens on proper behavior. Many of America's leaders are now acting just like King George III. These are challenging times in which to find agreement and consensus. History teaches us a tough lesson about this. Let's look back upon a newly formed nation that ignores heavenly wisdom.

CHAPTER 3

JUDGES

A New Country Example

What message has ever been sent to explain about the heavenly kingdom coexisting with a newly formed nation? Has God provided any instructions to citizens of heaven as to how to live in peace with others who drift away and only have knowledge of a national government? Let's reflect upon the history of the newly formed nation of Israel.

FROM JUDGES 2:1–5 (AUTHOR'S EMPHASIS):

The angel of the Lord went up from Gilgal to Bokim and said, "I brought you out of Egypt and led you into the land I swore to give to your ancestors. I said, 'I will never break my covenant with you, *and you shall not make a covenant with the people of this land, but you shall break down their altars.' Yet you have disobeyed me. Why have you done this? And I have also said, 'I will not drive them out before you; they will become traps for you, and their gods will become snares to you.'"*

When the angel of the Lord has spoken these things to all the Israelites, the people wept aloud, and they called that place Bokim. There they offered sacrifices to the Lord.

Israel had broken their covenant with the Lord. The angel of the Lord had helped Israel throw off the captivity of the Egyptian pharaohs, led them into a land given to them, and fought battles for them, and Israel failed to make the nation for the Lord—his desired portion on the earth which he created. The Lord still today has no nation in which to dwell in peace and without an abundance of conflict. He has no portion among all the nations on this earth. He is our Creator and author of life. We all should weep just as the Israelites did. Our Lord sits at the right hand of God waiting to return.

Judges reflect on mankind's best attempt to self-govern with the Lord's guidance. The book shows how the Lord was always faithful and raised up judges who were civic leaders to decide on the merits of Israel's cause to establish a nation where the Lord can reside in peace with his people. There were quite a few judges, some of the most famous were Deborah, Gideon, and Samson.

Unfortunately, at the end of the Book of Judges, Israel finally descends into civil war with the tribe of Benjamin being nearly completely destroyed, save for a remnant of 600. The issue that causes the civil war is strikingly similar to that of Lot living in Sodom—when certain citizens attacked messengers sent by God.

After the exodus from Egypt, after wandering forty years in the desert and relying on the Lord for provision, after receiving Moses and other priests and prophets, after being given the book of the law covenant, after entering a land given to them as the Lord leads the occupation and establishes a government—their final condition is like that of Lot who dwelt among pagan people who knew not the Lord. Who only lived by their own strength and had little or no knowledge of right from wrong. What an amazing heartbreak for the Lord. We indeed are weak in our flesh, but the Lord's strength is made perfect in weakness. Here are the final words to close the book of Judges.

From Judges 21:24–25:

At that time the Israelites left that place and went home to their tribes and clans, each to his own inheritance.

In those days Israel had no king; everyone did what as they saw fit.

In the books of Scripture that follow, Israel gets a national king. He is Saul from the tribe of Benjamin! How amazing is that! Israel asks for a national king to form a new secular government. The Lord is fired as their national king. In 1 Samuel, Israel gets a king like their neighboring nations. And that is still the way most people of the world see—only national governments. There are only national governments now governing the affairs of our world. Here are the words spoken by Jesus to Pilate of Rome.

FROM JOHN 18:36–40:

Jesus said, "My kingdom is not of this world. If it were, my servants would fight to prevent my arrest by the Jewish leaders. But now my kingdom is from another place."

"You are a king, then!" said Pilate.

Jesus answered, "You say that I am a king. In fact, the reason I was born and came into the world is to testify to the truth. Everyone on the side of truth listens to me."

"What is truth?" retorted Pilate. With this he went out again to the Jews gathered there and said, "I find no basis for a charge against him. But it is your custom for me to release to you one prisoner at the time of the Passover. Do you want me to release the 'the king of the Jews'?"

They shouted back, "No not him!"

We know with absolute certainty, Jesus has no place to "lay his head" in Israel as well as the natural world. But he does indwell us by his Spirit. We are his portion. We need to continue on his path of destiny. What will be the conclusion of this matter between two kingdoms?

CHAPTER 4

THE SUPREMACY
OF LAST ADAM

A Risen Jesus Reigns from Heaven

There are many scriptures that describe that the Lord promised to reign as king over Israel—and his faithfulness will continue until that day is fulfilled. As we wait upon that prophecy, many grafted in citizens of Gentile nations through faith have also become citizens of the kingdom of heaven. In all nations, believers can look forward to fulfilled and yet to be fulfilled prayers, blessings, and promises given to us by Jesus. Here are a few of them.

About the reign of David. From 2 Samuel 7:12–16:

"'When your days are over and you rest with your ancestors, I will raise up your offspring to succeed you, your own flesh and blood, and I will establish his kingdom. He is the one who will build a house for my Name, and I will establish the throne of his kingdom forever. I will be his father, and he will be my son. When he does wrong, I will punish him with a rod wielded by men, with floggings inflicted by human hands.

But my love will never be taken away from him, as I took it away from Saul, whom I removed from before you. Your house and your kingdom will endure forever before me; your throne will be established forever.'"

About power over nations. Psalm 2:1–9:

Why do the nations conspire and the peoples plot in vain? The kings of the earth rise up and the rulers band together against the Lord and against his anointed, saying, "Let us break their chains and throw off their shackles."

The One enthroned in heaven laughs; the Lord scoffs at them. He rebukes them in his anger and terrifies them in his wrath, saying, "I have installed my king on Zion, my holy mountain."

I will proclaim the Lord's decree:

He said to me, "You are my son; today I have become your father. Ask me, and I will make the nation's your inheritance, the ends of the earth your possession. You will break them with a rod of iron; you will dash them to pieces like pottery."

ABOUT THE REIGN OF DAVID. JEREMIAH 33:17–18:

"For this is what the Lord says: 'David will never fail to have a man to sit on the throne of Israel, nor will the Levitical priests ever fail to have a man to stand before me continually to offer burnt offerings, to burn grain offerings and to present sacrifices.'"

ABOUT JESUS RULING FROM HEAVEN. FROM ACTS 2:32–36:

God has raised this Jesus to life, and we are all witnesses of it. Exalted to the right hand of God, he has received from the Father the promised Holy Spirit and has poured out what you now see and hear. For David did not ascend to heaven, and yet he said,

"'The Lord said to my Lord: "Sit at my right hand until I make your enemies a footstool for your feet.'"'

"Therefore let all Israel be assured of this:

God has made this Jesus, whom you crucified, both Lord and Messiah."

With no portion among the nations, the risen king is now resting in heaven waiting to return. The reason for the wait is to permit things to run their course with the First Adam completing his mission.

CHAPTER 5

DESTINY

The Last Day Conditions

When does the nation of mankind, the First Adam, finally realize that there is a heavenly Last Adam whose kingdom reigns over the natural?

In the last days, the Lord decided to graciously help mankind develop a super world leader. He is a man that appears to have all the answers. He assumes the most power of anyone in world history. The Lord permits mankind a leader possessing deceptive godlike powers. All mankind will eventually have their choice of two kings. Either the one from earth who has become godlike and the other being the true choice of Jesus, the king seated in heaven, still on the throne at the right hand of God. People will need to choose wisely between these two kings.

FROM 2 THESSALONIANS 2:3–12:

Don't let anyone deceive you in any way, for that day will not come until the rebellion occurs and the man of lawlessness is revealed, the man doomed to destruction. He will oppose and will exalt himself over everything that is called God or is worshipped, so that he sets himself up in God's temple proclaiming himself to be God.

Don't you remember that when I was with you I used to tell you these things? And you now know what is holding him back, so that he may be revealed at the proper time. For the secret power of lawlessness is already at work; but the one who now holds it back will continue to do so till he is taken out of the way. And then the lawless one will be revealed, whom the Lord Jesus will overthrow with the breath of his mouth and destroy by the splendor of his coming. The coming of the lawless one will be in accordance of how Satan works. He will use all sorts of displays of power through signs and wonders that serve the lie, and all the ways that wickedness deceives those who are perishing. They perish because they refused to love the truth and so be saved. For this reason God sends them a powerful delusion so that they will believe the lie and that all will be condemned who have not believed the truth but have delighted in wickedness.

There is a time when the Last Adam will bring to a conclusion the dual rule of kingdoms. The kingdom rule of the First Adam ends badly. It must be dissolved after it fully matures and becomes headed by a supreme godlike leader. All his believers will be shut out of the heavenly kingdom of God. Now it's their turn to have no place on earth. Judgment finally comes with their right to choose another rival king.

And the Creator of all then has an unqualified right to judge. Please have mercy on us Lord.

CHAPTER 6

REFLECTIONS

Our Duty to the Last Adam

With no nation on earth to rule, Jesus is essentially now ruling from exile in the heavenly kingdom. The Bible does provide heavenly kingdom instruction to prepare for his return as king.

Citizens of the heavenly kingdom today have been charged with many duties. Paul, Peter, and John have written letters of instruction to church believers offering numerous corrections and encouragements. All cannot be discussed in this book. Firstly, the Holy Bible's New Testament contains every one of the essential obligations for living as a citizen of the kingdom of God. And secondly, churches have been established to worship, have fellowship, and conduct Bible study classes in order to provide instruction and to develop disciples. Citizens have opportunities for ample guidance on earth.

But thirdly, the best may be direct guidance from heaven, the personal indwelling of the Holy Spirit, also known as the Counselor. The wisdom of the Lord Almighty leaves a person speechless. There is simply nothing left to say about his wisdom, care, and love displayed by Jesus toward people on earth who are born of water and Spirit. Let's give an understanding of the need for the Holy Spirit by giving an example.

Suppose someone sends a life or death message to a multitude of people. Each person receives it differently. Some pay no attention, some hear it but misinterpret it, some catch it as intended and are able to warn others about their situation. What if the sender of the message has also the receiver of the message—an identical person to the sender? The receiver's job is to make certain the message is as accurately received as was sent. They always act in concert since they act as the same person. The intended audience is guided by both so as to clearly understand, so as to become an accurate disciple and witness of the message. Truth prevails!

FROM JOHN 16:12–15:

"I have much more to say to you, more than you can now bear. But when he, the Spirit of truth, comes, he will guide you into all truth. He will not speak on his own; he will speak only what he hears, and he will tell you what is yet to come. He will glorify me because it is from me that he will receive what he will make known to you. All that belongs to the Father is mine. That is why I said the Spirit will receive from me what he will make known to you."

True believers are bounded like Israel was by twin pillars while in the desert. Citizen disciples are instructed to stay contained in the boundaries that Jesus has established for each heavenly kingdom citizen. Otherwise, having lost connection with the will of Jesus, their efforts are not supported by him.

FROM JOHN 15:1–12 (AUTHOR'S EMPHASIS):

"I am the true vine, and my Father is the gardener. He cuts off every branch in me that bears no fruit, while every branch that does not bear fruit he prunes so that it will be even more fruitful. You are already clean because of the word I have spoken to you. Remain in me, as I also remain in you. *No branch can bear fruit you itself; it must remain in the vine. Neither can you bear fruit unless you remain in me.*

"I am the vine; you are the branches. If you remain in me and I in you, you will bear much fruit; apart from me you can do nothing. If you do not remain in me, you are like a branch that is thrown away and withers; such branches are picked up, thrown into the fire and burned. If you remain in me and my words remain in you, ask whatever you wish, and it will be done for you. This is to my Father's glory, that you bear much fruit, showing yourselves to be my disciples.

"As the Father has loved me, so have I loved you. Now remain in my love. If you keep my commands, you will remain in my love, just as I have kept my Father's commands and remain in his love. I have told you this so that my joy may be in you and that your joy may be complete. My command is this: Love each other as I have loved you."

Believers in the Last Adam are to act in love and unity, not becoming divisive, pitting one group against another. Drowning it's citizens in conflict.

CHAPTER 7

OUR STRUGGLE

Spiritual Fortitude

Wisdom is given to us freely by the Lord. In order for American citizens to continue to be blessed, they need the wisdom of God.

Many things claimed by America's leaders of today are acting independently of God's. They are the First Adam national government that offer up burdensome and unworkable short-term solutions to the before mentioned issues noted in Chapter 2. This confuses many citizens to focus on problems and offer little workable solutions. America will go bankrupt and descend into greater polarization if their power-seeking intentions become reality. And their solutions offer no permanent resolutions, only short-term appeasement.

Although God stands ready to provide wisdom, power, blessings, grace, and his love, those who have no citizenship in his kingdom press forward without him. They think themselves capable of regulating Americans with only laws. As we see from history, God's involvement in America is essential for its success. But, somehow, the First Adam American struggles to invite him into their schools, holidays, courtrooms, politics, etc. God laughs at such arrogance.

American citizens who belong to both the First Adam and the Last Adam need to pray for productive and insightful leadership. We also need to pray for agreement among our leaders. Let's be resolute in inviting the all-powerful God to will and bring his kingdom into our lives. He is our comforter, provider, and healer!

FROM 2 TIMOTHY 3:1–5 (AUTHOR'S EMPHASIS):

But mark this: There will be terrible times in the last days. People will be lovers of themselves, lovers of money, boastful, proud, abusive, disobedient to their parents, ungrateful, unholy, without love, unforgiving, slanderous, without self-control, brutal, not lovers of the good, treacherous, rash, conceited, lovers of pleasure rather than lovers of God—having a form of godliness but denying its power. *Have nothing to do with such people.*

Now there is some good advice. Believers and citizens of the heavenly kingdom, whose king is of the Last Adam, should not give authority to such people if they expect to live peaceably in America while pursuing life, liberty, and happiness. These types of people may appear to have a just cause, but they lack the civility which is essential to govern all America. Civility trumps diversified identity politics. Every American that claims dual kingdom citizenship needs to expect better behavior from their elected leaders.

Dual citizens should become informed about a candidate's viewpoint in supporting America's founding beliefs. These people profess to uphold them, but they will not once in office.

May God bless America!

9 781400 328895